Travel phrasebooks collection
«Everything Will Be Okay!»

PHRASEBOOK

DUTCH

By Andrey Taranov

THE MOST IMPORTANT PHRASES

This phrasebook contains the most important phrases and questions for basic communication Everything you need to survive overseas

T&P BOOKS

Phrasebook + 250-word dictionary

English-Dutch phrasebook & mini dictionary

By Andrey Taranov

The collection of "Everything Will Be Okay" travel phrasebooks published by T&P Books is designed for people traveling abroad for tourism and business. The phrasebooks contain what matters most - the essentials for basic communication. This is an indispensable set of phrases to "survive" while abroad.

You'll also find a mini dictionary with 250 useful words required for everyday communication - the names of months and days of the week, measurements, family members, and more.

T&P Books Publishing
www.tpbooks.com

ISBN: 978-1-78492-421-8

This book is also available in E-book formats.
Please visit www.tpbooks.com or the major online bookstores.

FOREWORD

The collection of "Everything Will Be Okay" travel phrasebooks published by T&P Books is designed for people traveling abroad for tourism and business. The phrasebooks contain what matters most - the essentials for basic communication. This is an indispensable set of phrases to "survive" while abroad.

This phrasebook will help you in most cases where you need to ask something, get directions, find out how much something costs, etc. It can also resolve difficult communication situations where gestures just won't help.

This book contains a lot of phrases that have been grouped according to the most relevant topics. You'll also find a mini dictionary with useful words - numbers, time, calendar, colors...

Take "Everything Will Be Okay" phrasebook with you on the road and you'll have an irreplaceable traveling companion who will help you find your way out of any situation and teach you to not fear speaking with foreigners.

TABLE OF CONTENTS

Pronunciation 5
List of abbreviations 7
English-Dutch 9
Mini Dictionary 73

T&P Books Publishing

PRONUNCIATION

Letter	Dutch example	T&P phonetic alphabet	English example

Consonants

Letter	Dutch example	T&P phonetic alphabet	English example
B b	boek	[b]	baby, book
C c	cosmetica	[k]	clock, kiss
C c [1]	procedure	[s]	city, boss
D d	doek	[d]	day, doctor
F f	fazant	[f]	face, food
G g	groen	[g]	game, gold
H h	helder	[ɦ]	huge, humor
J j	jong	[j]	yes, New York
K k	kip	[k]	clock, kiss
L l	long	[l]	lace, people
M m	mens	[m]	magic, milk
N n	neus	[n]	name, normal
P p	pony	[p]	pencil, private
Q q	qwerty	[k]	clock, kiss
R r	reus	[r]	rolled [r]
S s	som	[s]	city, boss
T t	tijger	[t]	tourist, trip
V v	vink	[ʋ]	vase, winter
W w	worm	[w]	vase, winter
X x	xylofoon	[ks]	box, taxi
Z z	zebra	[z]	zebra, please
sch	schoen	[sh]	racehorse
ch	lach	[h]	home, have
ng	koning	[ŋ]	English, ring

Letter	Dutch example	T&P phonetic alphabet	English example

Vowels and diphthongs

A a	**as**	[ɑ]	shorter than in park, card
aa	**haas**	[ɑ:]	father, answer
E e	**zeker**	[ɛ]	man, bad
I i	**wit**	[ɪ], [i]	tin, see
O o	**bok**	[ɔ]	bottle, doctor
oo	**groot**	[ɔ:]	door, floor
U u	**rund**	[y]	fuel, tuna
uu	**minuut**	[y:]	longer than fuel
Y y	**xylofoon**	[i:]	feet, meter
au	**blauw**	[aʊ]	now, down
eu	**neus**	[ø]	eternal, church
oe	**kalkoen**	[ʊ]	good, booklet
ei	**ei**	[ɛj]	aim, play
ij	**ijsje**	[ɛj]	aim, play
ie	**pier**	[i]	shorter than in feet

Comments

[1] before e, i, y

LIST OF ABBREVIATIONS

English abbreviations

ab.	-	about
adj	-	adjective
adv	-	adverb
anim.	-	animate
as adj	-	attributive noun used as adjective
e.g.	-	for example
etc.	-	et cetera
fam.	-	familiar
fem.	-	feminine
form.	-	formal
inanim.	-	inanimate
masc.	-	masculine
math	-	mathematics
mil.	-	military
n	-	noun
pl	-	plural
pron.	-	pronoun
sb	-	somebody
sing.	-	singular
sth	-	something
v aux	-	auxiliary verb
vi	-	intransitive verb
vi, vt	-	intransitive, transitive verb
vt	-	transitive verb

Dutch abbreviations

mv.	-	plural

Dutch articles

de	-	common gender
de/het	-	neuter, common gender
het	-	neuter

DUTCH PHRASEBOOK

This section contains important phrases that may come in handy in various real-life situations.
The phrasebook will help you ask for directions, clarify a price, buy tickets, and order food at a restaurant

T&P Books Publishing

PHRASEBOOK CONTENTS

The bare minimum 12
Questions 15
Needs 16
Asking for directions 18
Signs 20
Transportation. General phrases 22
Buying tickets 24
Bus 26
Train 28
On the train. Dialogue (No ticket) 29
Taxi 30
Hotel 32
Restaurant 35
Shopping 37
In town 39
Money 41

Time 43
Greetings. Introductions 45
Farewells 47
Foreign language 49
Apologies 50
Agreement 51
Refusal. Expressing doubt 52
Expressing gratitude 54
Congratulations. Best wishes 55
Socializing 56
Sharing impressions. Emotions 59
Problems. Accidents 61
Health problems 64
At the pharmacy 67
The bare minimum 69

T&P Books Publishing

The bare minimum

Excuse me, …	**Pardon, …** [par'dɔn, …]
Hello.	**Hallo.** ['halɔ]
Thank you.	**Bedankt.** [bə'dankt]
Good bye.	**Tot ziens.** [tɔt zins]
Yes.	**Ja.** [ja]
No.	**Nee.** [ne:]
I don't know.	**Ik weet het niet.** [ik we:t ət nit]
Where? | Where to? | When?	**Waar? | Waarheen? | Wanneer?** [wa:r? | wa:r'he:n? | wa'ne:r?]

I need …	**Ik heb … nodig** [ik hɛp … 'nɔdəx]
I want …	**Ik wil …** [ik wil …]
Do you have …?	**Hebt u …?** [hɛpt ju …?]
Is there a … here?	**Is hier een …?** [is hir en …?]
May I …?	**Mag ik …?** [max ik …?]
…, please (polite request)	**… alstublieft** [… alsty'blift]

I'm looking for …	**Ik zoek …** [ik zuk …]
restroom	**toilet** [twa'lɛt]
ATM	**geldautomaat** [xɛlt autɔ'ma:t]
pharmacy (drugstore)	**apotheek** [apɔ'te:k]
hospital	**ziekenhuis** ['zikənhœys]
police station	**politiebureau** [pɔ'litsi by'rɔ]
subway	**metro** ['metrɔ]

taxi	**taxi** ['taksi]
train station	**station** [sta'sʲɔn]
My name is …	**Ik heet …** [ik he:t …]
What's your name?	**Hoe heet u?** [hu he:t ju?]
Could you please help me?	**Kunt u me helpen alstublieft?** [kynt ju mə 'hɛlpən alsty'blift?]
I've got a problem.	**Ik heb een probleem.** [ik hɛp en prɔ'ble:m]
I don't feel well.	**Ik voel me niet goed.** [ik vul mə nit xut]
Call an ambulance!	**Bel een ambulance!** [bɛl en amby'lansə!]
May I make a call?	**Mag ik opbellen?** [max ik ɔ'bɛlən?]
I'm sorry.	**Sorry.** ['sɔri]
You're welcome.	**Graag gedaan.** [xra:x xə'da:n]
I, me	**Ik, mij** [ik, mɛj]
you (inform.)	**jij** [jɛj]
he	**hij** [hɛj]
she	**zij** [zɛj]
they (masc.)	**zij** [zɛj]
they (fem.)	**zij** [zɛj]
we	**wij** [wɛj]
you (pl)	**jullie** ['juli]
you (sg, form.)	**u** [ju]
ENTRANCE	**INGANG** ['inxaŋ]
EXIT	**UITGANG** ['œytxaŋ]
OUT OF ORDER	**BUITEN GEBRUIK** ['bœytən xə'brœyk]
CLOSED	**GESLOTEN** [xə'slɔtən]

OPEN	**OPEN** ['ɔpən]
FOR WOMEN	**DAMES** ['daməs]
FOR MEN	**HEREN** ['herən]

Questions

Where?	**Waar?** [wa:r?]
Where to?	**Waarheen?** [wa:r'he:n?]
Where from?	**Vanwaar?** [van'wa:r?]
Why?	**Waar?** [wa:r?]
For what reason?	**Waarom?** [wa:'rɔm?]
When?	**Wanneer?** [wa'ne:r?]

How long?	**Hoe lang?** [hu laŋ?]
At what time?	**Hoe laat?** [hu la:t?]
How much?	**Hoeveel?** ['huve:l?]
Do you have ...?	**Hebt u ...?** [hɛpt ju ...?]
Where is ...?	**Waar is ...?** [wa:r is ...?]

What time is it?	**Hoe laat is het?** [hu la:t is ət?]
May I make a call?	**Mag ik opbellen?** [max ik ɔ'bɛlən?]
Who's there?	**Wie is daar?** [wi is da:r?]
Can I smoke here?	**Mag ik hier roken?** [max ik hir 'rɔkən?]
May I ...?	**Mag ik ...?** [max ik ...?]

Needs

I'd like ...	**Ik zou graag ...** [ik 'zau xra:x ...]
I don't want ...	**Ik wil niet ...** [ik wil nit ...]
I'm thirsty.	**Ik heb dorst.** [ik hɛp dɔrst]
I want to sleep.	**Ik wil gaan slapen.** [ik wil xa:n 'slapən]
I want ...	**Ik wil ...** [ik wil ...]
to wash up	**wassen** ['wasən]
to brush my teeth	**mijn tanden poetsen** [mɛjn 'tandən 'putsən]
to rest a while	**even rusten** ['evən 'rystən]
to change my clothes	**me omkleden** [mə 'ɔmkledən]
to go back to the hotel	**teruggaan naar het hotel** [tə'ryxxa:n na:r hɛt hɔ'tɛl]
to buy ...	**... kopen** [... 'kɔpən]
to go to ...	**gaan naar ...** [xa:n na:r ...]
to visit ...	**bezoeken ...** [bə'zukən ...]
to meet with ...	**ontmoeten ...** [ɔnt'mutən ...]
to make a call	**opbellen** [ɔ'bɛlən]
I'm tired.	**Ik ben moe.** [ik bɛn mu]
We are tired.	**We zijn moe.** [we zɛjn mu]
I'm cold.	**Ik heb het koud.** [ik hɛp ət 'kaut]
I'm hot.	**Ik heb het warm.** [ik hɛp ət warm]
I'm OK.	**Ik ben okay.** [ik bɛn ɔ'kɛj]

I need to make a call.	**Ik moet opbellen.** [ik mut ɔ'bɛlən]
I need to go to the restroom.	**Ik moet naar het toilet.** [ik mut nɑ:r ət twɑ'lɛt]
I have to go.	**Ik moet weg.** [ik mut wɛx]
I have to go now.	**Ik moet nu weg.** [ik mut ny wɛx]

Asking for directions

Excuse me, ...	**Pardon, ...** [pɑr'dɔn, ...]
Where is ...?	**Waar is ...?** [wa:r is ...?]
Which way is ...?	**Welke richting is ...?** ['wɛlkə 'rixtiŋ is ...?]
Could you help me, please?	**Kunt u me helpen alstublieft?** [kynt ju mə 'hɛlpən ɑlsty'blift?]
I'm looking for ...	**Ik zoek ...** [ik zuk ...]
I'm looking for the exit.	**Waar is de uitgang?** [wa:r is də 'œytxɑŋ?]
I'm going to ...	**Ik ga naar ...** [ik xɑ na:r ...]
Am I going the right way to ...?	**Is dit de weg naar ...?** [is dit də wɛx na:r ...?]
Is it far?	**Is het ver?** [iz ət vɛr?]
Can I get there on foot?	**Kan ik er lopend naar toe?** [kɑn ik ɛr 'lɔpənt na:r tu?]
Can you show me on the map?	**Kunt u het op de plattegrond aanwijzen?** [kynt ju ət ɔp de plɑtə'xrɔnt 'a:nwɛjzən?]
Show me where we are right now.	**Kunt u me aanwijzen waar we nu zijn?** [kynt ju mə 'a:nwɛjzən wa:r wə ny zɛjn]
Here	**Hier** [hir]
There	**Daar** [da:r]
This way	**Deze kant uit** ['dezə kɑnt 'œyt]
Turn right.	**Rechtsaf.** [rɛxts'ɑf]
Turn left.	**Linksaf.** ['linksɑf]
first (second, third) turn	**eerste (tweede, derde) bocht** ['ɛ:rstə ('twe:də, 'dɛrdə) bɔxt]
to the right	**rechtsaf** [rɛxts'ɑf]

to the left	**linksaf** ['linksɑf]
Go straight.	**Ga rechtuit.** [xɑ 'rɛxtœyt]

Signs

WELCOME!	**WELKOM!** ['wɛlkɔm!]
ENTRANCE	**INGANG** ['inxɑŋ]
EXIT	**UITGANG** ['œytxɑŋ]
PUSH	**DRUK** [dryk]
PULL	**TREK** [trɛk]
OPEN	**OPEN** ['ɔpən]
CLOSED	**GESLOTEN** [xə'slɔtən]
FOR WOMEN	**DAMES** ['dɑməs]
FOR MEN	**HEREN** ['herən]
MEN, GENTS	**HEREN (M)** ['herən]
WOMEN, LADIES	**DAMES (V)** ['dɑməs]
DISCOUNTS	**KORTINGEN** ['kɔrtiŋən]
SALE	**UITVERKOOP** [œyt'vɛrkɔ:p]
FREE	**GRATIS** ['xrɑtis]
NEW!	**NIEUW!** [niu!]
ATTENTION!	**PAS OP!** [pɑs ɔp!]
NO VACANCIES	**ALLE KAMERS BEZET** ['ɑle 'kɑmərs bə'zɛt]
RESERVED	**GERESERVEERD** [xərezɛr've:rt]
ADMINISTRATION	**ADMINISTRATIE** [ɑdminist'rɑtsi]
STAFF ONLY	**UITSLUITEND PERSONEEL** ['œytslœytənt pɛrsɔ'ne:l]

BEWARE OF THE DOG!	**PAS OP VOOR DE HOND!** [pas ɔp vɔ:r də hɔnt!]
NO SMOKING!	**VERBODEN TE ROKEN!** [vər'bɔdən tə 'rɔkən!]
DO NOT TOUCH!	**NIET AANRAKEN!** [nit 'a:nrakən!]
DANGEROUS	**GEVAARLIJK** [xe'va:rlək]
DANGER	**GEVAAR** [xe'va:r]
HIGH VOLTAGE	**HOOGSPANNING** [hɔ:xs'paniŋ]
NO SWIMMING!	**VERBODEN TE ZWEMMEN** [vər'bɔdən tə 'zwemən]

OUT OF ORDER	**BUITEN GEBRUIK** ['bœytən xə'brœyk]
FLAMMABLE	**ONTVLAMBAAR** [ɔnt'flamba:r]
FORBIDDEN	**VERBODEN** [vər'bɔdən]
NO TRESPASSING!	**VERBODEN TOEGANG** [vər'bɔdən 'tuxaŋ]
WET PAINT	**NATTE VERF** ['natə vɛrf]

CLOSED FOR RENOVATIONS	**GESLOTEN WEGENS VERBOUWING** [xə'slɔtən 'wexəns vər'bauwiŋ]
WORKS AHEAD	**WERK IN UITVOERING** [wɛrk in œyt'vuriŋ]
DETOUR	**OMWEG** ['ɔmwɛx]

Transportation. General phrases

plane	**vliegtuig** ['vlixtœyx]
train	**trein** [trɛjn]
bus	**bus** [bys]
ferry	**veerpont** ['ve:rpɔnt]
taxi	**taxi** ['taksi]
car	**auto** ['autɔ]
schedule	**dienstregeling** ['dinstrexəliŋ]
Where can I see the schedule?	**Waar is de dienstregeling?** [wa:r is də dinst'rexəliŋ?]
workdays (weekdays)	**werkdagen** [wɛrk'daxən]
weekends	**weekends** ['wi:kɛnts]
holidays	**vakanties** [va'kantsis]
DEPARTURE	**VERTREK** [vər'trɛk]
ARRIVAL	**AANKOMST** ['a:nkɔmst]
DELAYED	**VERTRAAGD** [vərt'ra:xt]
CANCELED	**GEANNULEERD** [xəany'le:rt]
next (train, etc.)	**volgende** ['vɔlxəndə]
first	**eerste** ['ɛ:rstə]
last	**laatste** ['la:tstə]
When is the next ...?	**Hoe laat gaat de volgende ...?** [hu la:t xa:t də 'vɔlxəndə ...?]
When is the first ...?	**Hoe laat gaat de eerste ...?** [hu la:t xa:t də 'ɛ:rstə ...?]

When is the last ...?	**Hoe laat gaat de laatste ...?** [hu la:t xa:t də 'la:tstə ...?]
transfer (change of trains, etc.)	**aansluiting** ['a:nslœytiŋ]
to make a transfer	**overstappen** [ɔvər'stapən]
Do I need to make a transfer?	**Moet ik overstappen?** [mut ik ɔvər'stapən?]

Buying tickets

Where can I buy tickets?	**Waar kan ik kaartjes kopen?** [wa:r kan ik 'ka:rtʲəs 'kɔpən?]
ticket	**kaartje** ['ka:rtʲə]
to buy a ticket	**een kaartje kopen** [en 'ka:rtʲə 'kɔpən]
ticket price	**prijs van een kaartje** [prɛjs van en 'ka:rtʲə]
Where to?	**Waarheen?** [wa:r'he:n?]
To what station?	**Naar welk station?** [na:r wɛlk sta'sʲɔn?]
I need ...	**Ik heb ... nodig** [ik hɛp ... 'nɔdəx]
one ticket	**een kaartje** [en 'ka:rtʲə]
two tickets	**twee kaartjes** [twe: 'ka:rtʲəs]
three tickets	**drie kaartjes** [dri 'ka:rtʲəs]
one-way	**enkel** ['ɛnkəl]
round-trip	**retour** [re'tu:r]
first class	**eerste klas** ['ɛ:rstə klas]
second class	**tweede klas** ['twe:də klas]
today	**vandaag** [van'da:x]
tomorrow	**morgen** ['mɔrxən]
the day after tomorrow	**overmorgen** [ɔvər'mɔrxən]
in the morning	**s morgens** [s 'mɔrxəns]
in the afternoon	**s middags** [s 'midaxs]
in the evening	**s avonds** [s 'avɔnts]

aisle seat	**zitplaats aan het gangpad** ['zitpla:ʦ a:n ət 'xaŋpat]
window seat	**zitplaats bij het raam** ['zitpla:ʦ bɛj ət ra:m]
How much?	**Hoeveel?** ['huve:l?]
Can I pay by credit card?	**Kan ik met een creditcard betalen?** [kan ik mɛt en 'kredit kart bə'talən?]

Bus

bus	**bus** [bys]
intercity bus	**intercity bus** [inter'siti bys]
bus stop	**bushalte** [bys'haltə]
Where's the nearest bus stop?	**Waar is de meest nabij gelegen bushalte?** [wa:r is də me:st na'bɛj xə'lexən bys'haltə?]
number (bus ~, etc.)	**nummer** ['nymər]
Which bus do I take to get to ...?	**Met welke bus kan ik naar ... gaan?** [mɛt 'wɛlkə bys kan ik na:r ... xa:n?]
Does this bus go to ...?	**Gaat deze bus naar ...?** [xa:t 'dezə bys na:r ...?]
How frequent are the buses?	**Hoe dikwijls rijden de bussen?** [hu 'dikwəls 'rɛjdən də 'bysən?]
every 15 minutes	**om het kwartier** [ɔm ət kwar'tir]
every half hour	**om het half uur** [ɔm ət half y:r]
every hour	**om het uur** [ɔm ət y:r]
several times a day	**verschillende keren per dag** [vərs'xiləndə 'kerən pər dax]
... times a day	**... keer per dag** [... ke:r pər dax]
schedule	**dienstregeling** ['dinstrexəliŋ]
Where can I see the schedule?	**Waar is de dienstregeling?** [wa:r is də dinst'rexəliŋ?]
When is the next bus?	**Hoe laat vertrekt de volgende bus?** [hu la:t vər'trɛkt də 'vɔlxəndə bys?]
When is the first bus?	**Hoe laat vertrekt de eerste bus?** [hu la:t vər'trɛkt də 'ɛ:rstə bys?]
When is the last bus?	**Hoe laat vertrekt de laatste bus?** [hu la:t vər'trɛkt də 'la:tstə bys?]
stop	**halte** ['haltə]

next stop	**volgende halte** ['vɔlxəndə 'haltə]
last stop (terminus)	**eindstation** [ɛjnt sta'sʲɔn]
Stop here, please.	**Hier stoppen alstublieft.** [hir 'stɔpən alsty'blift]
Excuse me, this is my stop.	**Pardon, dit is mijn halte.** [par'dɔn, dit is mɛjn 'haltə]

Train

train	**trein** [trɛjn]
suburban train	**pendeltrein** ['pendəl trɛjn]
long-distance train	**langeafstandstrein** ['laŋe 'afstanʦ trɛjn]
train station	**station** [sta'sʲɔn]
Excuse me, where is the exit to the platform?	**Pardon, waar is de toegang tot het perron?** [par'dɔn, wa:r is də 'tuxaŋ tɔt ət pɛ'rɔn?]
Does this train go to ...?	**Gaat deze trein naar ...?** [xa:t 'dezə trɛjn na:r ...?]
next train	**volgende trein** ['vɔlxəndə trɛjn]
When is the next train?	**Hoe laat gaat de volgende trein?** [hu la:t xa:t də 'vɔlxəndə trɛjn?]
Where can I see the schedule?	**Waar is de dienstregeling?** [wa:r is də dinst'rexəliŋ?]
From which platform?	**Van welk perron?** [van wɛlk pɛ'rɔn?]
When does the train arrive in ...?	**Wanneer komt de trein aan in ...?** [wa'ne:r kɔmt də trɛjn a:n in ...?]
Please help me.	**Kunt u me helpen alstublieft?** [kynt ju mə 'hɛlpən alsty'blift?]
I'm looking for my seat.	**Ik zoek mijn zitplaats.** [ik zuk mɛjn 'zitpla:ʦ]
We're looking for our seats.	**Wij zoeken onze zitplaatsen.** [wɛj 'zukən 'ɔnzə 'zitpla:ʦən]
My seat is taken.	**Mijn zitplaats is bezet.** [mɛjn 'zitpla:ʦ is bə'zɛt]
Our seats are taken.	**Onze zitplaatsen zijn bezet.** ['ɔnzə 'zitpla:ʦən zɛjn bə'zɛt]
I'm sorry but this is my seat.	**Sorry, maar dit is mijn zitplaats.** ['sɔri, ma:r dit is mɛjn 'zitpla:ʦ]
Is this seat taken?	**Is deze zitplaats bezet?** [is 'dezə 'zitpla:ʦ bə'zɛt?]
May I sit here?	**Mag ik hier zitten?** [max ik hir 'zitən?]

On the train. Dialogue (No ticket)

Ticket, please.	**Uw kaartje alstublieft.** [yw 'ka:rtʲə alsty'blift]
I don't have a ticket.	**Ik heb geen kaartje.** [ik hɛp xe:n 'ka:rtʲə]
I lost my ticket.	**Ik heb mijn kaartje verloren.** [ik hɛp mɛjn 'ka:rtʲə vər'lɔrən]
I forgot my ticket at home.	**Ik heb mijn kaartje thuis vergeten.** [ik hɛp mɛjn 'ka:rtʲə thœys vər'xetən]
You can buy a ticket from me.	**U kunt een kaartje van mij kopen.** [ju kynt en 'ka:rtʲə van mɛj 'kɔpən]
You will also have to pay a fine.	**U moet ook een boete betalen.** [ju mut ɔ:k en 'butə bə'talən]
Okay.	**Okay.** [ɔ'kɛj]
Where are you going?	**Waar gaat u naartoe?** [wa:r xa:t ju na:rtu?]
I'm going to ...	**Ik ga naar ...** [ik xa na:r ...]
How much? I don't understand.	**Hoeveel kost het? Ik versta het niet.** ['huve:l kɔst ət? ik vərs'ta ət nit]
Write it down, please.	**Schrijf het neer alstublieft.** [sxrɛjf ət ne:r alsty'blift]
Okay. Can I pay with a credit card?	**Okay. Kan ik met een creditcard betalen?** [ɔ'kɛj. kan ik mɛt en 'kredit kart bə'talən?]
Yes, you can.	**Ja, dat kan.** [ja, dat kan]
Here's your receipt.	**Hier is uw ontvangstbewijs.** [hir is yw ɔnt'faŋst bə'wɛjs]
Sorry about the fine.	**Sorry voor de boete.** ['sɔri vɔ:r də 'butə]
That's okay. It was my fault.	**Maakt niet uit. Het is mijn schuld.** [ma:kt nit œyt hɛt is mɛjn sxylt]
Enjoy your trip.	**Prettige reis.** ['prɛtixə rɛjs]

Taxi

taxi	**taxi** ['taksi]
taxi driver	**taxi chauffeur** ['taksi ʃɔ'før]
to catch a taxi	**een taxi nemen** [en 'taksi 'nemən]
taxi stand	**taxistandplaats** ['taksi 'stantpla:ʦ]
Where can I get a taxi?	**Waar kan ik een taxi nemen?** [wa:r kan ik en 'taksi 'nemən?]
to call a taxi	**een taxi bellen** [en 'taksi 'bɛlən]
I need a taxi.	**Ik heb een taxi nodig.** [ik hɛp en 'taksi 'nɔdəx]
Right now.	**Nu onmiddellijk.** [ny ɔn'midələk]
What is your address (location)?	**Wat is uw adres?** [wat is yw ad'rɛs?]
My address is …	**Mijn adres is …** [mɛjn ad'rɛs is …]
Your destination?	**Uw bestemming?** [yw bəs'tɛmiŋ?]
Excuse me, …	**Pardon, …** [par'dɔn, …]
Are you available?	**Bent u vrij?** [bɛnt ju vrɛj?]
How much is it to get to …?	**Hoeveel kost het naar …?** ['huve:l kɔst ət na:r …?]
Do you know where it is?	**Weet u waar dit is?** [we:t ju wa:r dit is?]
Airport, please.	**Luchthaven alstublieft.** [lyxt'havən alsty'blift]
Stop here, please.	**Hier stoppen alstublieft.** [hir 'stɔpən alsty'blift]
It's not here.	**Het is niet hier.** [hɛt is nit hir]
This is the wrong address.	**Dit is het verkeerde adres.** [dit is ət vər'ke:rdə ad'rɛs]
Turn left.	**Linksaf.** ['linksaf]
Turn right.	**Rechtsaf.** [rɛxʦ'af]

How much do I owe you?	**Hoeveel ben ik u schuldig?** ['huve:l bεn ik ju 'sxyldəx?]
I'd like a receipt, please.	**Kan ik een bon krijgen alstublieft.** [kan ik en bɔn 'krεjxən alsty'blift]
Keep the change.	**Hou het kleingeld maar.** ['hau ət 'klεjnxεlt ma:r]

Would you please wait for me?	**Wil u even op mij wachten?** [wil ju 'evən ɔp mεj 'waxtən?]
five minutes	**vijf minuten** [vεjf mi'nytən]
ten minutes	**tien minuten** [tin mi'nytən]
fifteen minutes	**vijftien minuten** ['vεjftin mi'nytən]
twenty minutes	**twintig minuten** ['twintəx mi'nytən]
half an hour	**een half uur** [en half y:r]

Hotel

Hello.	**Hallo.** ['halɔ]
My name is …	**Ik heet …** [ik he:t …]
I have a reservation.	**Ik heb gereserveerd.** [ik hɛp xərezɛr've:rt]
I need …	**Ik heb … nodig** [ik hɛp … 'nɔdəx]
a single room	**een enkele kamer** [en 'ɛnkelə 'kamər]
a double room	**een tweepersoons kamer** [en twe:pɛr'sɔ:ns 'kamər]
How much is that?	**Hoeveel kost dat?** ['huve:l kɔst dat?]
That's a bit expensive.	**Dat is nogal duur.** [dat is 'nɔxal dy:r]
Do you have any other options?	**Zijn er geen andere mogelijkheden?** [zɛjn ɛr xe:n 'anderə 'mɔxələkhedən?]
I'll take it.	**Die neem ik.** [di ne:m ik]
I'll pay in cash.	**Ik betaal contant.** [ik bə'ta:l kɔn'tant]
I've got a problem.	**Ik heb een probleem.** [ik hɛp en prɔ'ble:m]
My … is broken.	**Mijn … is stuk.** [mɛjn … is styk]
My … is out of order.	**Mijn … doet het niet meer.** [mɛjn … dut ət nit me:r]
TV	**TV** [te've]
air conditioning	**airco** ['ɛrkɔ]
tap	**kraan** [kra:n]
shower	**douche** [duʃ]
sink	**lavabo** [lava'bɔ]
safe	**brandkast** ['brantkast]

door lock	**deurslot** ['dørslɔt]
electrical outlet	**stopcontact** ['stɔp kɔn'tɑkt]
hairdryer	**haardroger** ['hɑ:rdrɔxər]

I don't have …	**Ik heb geen …** [ik hɛp xe:n …]
water	**water** ['watər]
light	**licht** [lixt]
electricity	**stroom** [strɔ:m]

Can you give me …?	**Kunt u mij een … bezorgen?** [kynt ju mɛj en … bə'zɔrxən?]
a towel	**een handdoek** [en 'hɑnduk]
a blanket	**een deken** [en 'dekən]
slippers	**pantoffels** [pɑn'tɔfəls]
a robe	**een badjas** [en bɑdjɑs]
shampoo	**shampoo** ['ʃʌmpɔ:]
soap	**zeep** [ze:p]

I'd like to change rooms.	**Ik wil van kamer veranderen.** [ik wil vɑn 'kɑmər və'rɑnderən]
I can't find my key.	**Ik kan mijn sleutel niet vinden.** [ik kɑn mɛjn 'sløtel nit 'vindən]
Could you open my room, please?	**Kunt u mijn kamer openen alstublieft?** [kynt ju mɛjn 'kɑmər 'ɔpenən ɑlsty'blift?]
Who's there?	**Wie is daar?** [wi is dɑ:r?]
Come in!	**Kom binnen!** [kɔm 'binən!]
Just a minute!	**Een ogenblikje!** [en 'ɔxənblikje!]
Not right now, please.	**Niet op dit moment alstublieft.** [nit ɔp dit mɔ'mɛnt ɑlsty'blift]

Come to my room, please.	**Kom naar mijn kamer alstublieft.** [kɔm nɑ:r mɛjn 'kɑmər ɑlsty'blift]
I'd like to order food service.	**Kan ik room service krijgen.** [kɑn ik rɔ:m 'sø:rvis 'krɛjxən]
My room number is …	**Mijn kamernummer is …** [mɛjn 'kɑmər 'nymer is …]

I'm leaving ...	**Ik vertrek ...** [ik vər'trɛk ...]
We're leaving ...	**Wij vertrekken ...** [wɛj vər'trɛkən ...]
right now	**nu onmiddellijk** [ny ɔn'midələk]
this afternoon	**vanmiddag** [van'midax]
tonight	**vanavond** [va'navɔnt]
tomorrow	**morgen** ['mɔrxən]
tomorrow morning	**morgenochtend** ['mɔrxən 'ɔxtənt]
tomorrow evening	**morgenavond** ['mɔrxən 'avɔnt]
the day after tomorrow	**overmorgen** [ɔvər'mɔrxən]

I'd like to pay.	**Ik zou willen afrekenen.** [ik 'zau 'wilən 'afrekənən]
Everything was wonderful.	**Alles was uitstekend.** ['aləs was œyts'tekənt]
Where can I get a taxi?	**Waar kan ik een taxi nemen?** [wa:r kan ik en 'taksi 'nemən?]
Would you call a taxi for me, please?	**Wil u alstublieft een taxi bestellen?** [wil ju alsty'blift en 'taksi bəs'tɛlən?]

Restaurant

Can I look at the menu, please?	**Kan ik het menu zien alstublieft?** [kan ik ət me'ny zin alsty'blift?]
Table for one.	**Een tafel voor één persoon.** [en 'tafəl vɔ:r en pɛr'sɔ:n]
There are two (three, four) of us.	**We zijn met z'n tweeën (drieën, vieren).** [we zɛjn mɛt zən 'twe:ɛn ('driɛn, 'virən)]
Smoking	**Roken** ['rɔkən]
No smoking	**Niet roken** [nit 'rɔkən]
Excuse me! (addressing a waiter)	**Hallo! Pardon!** ['halɔ! par'dɔn!]
menu	**menu** [me'ny]
wine list	**wijnkaart** ['wɛjnka:rt]
The menu, please.	**Het menu alstublieft.** [hɛt me'ny alsty'blift]
Are you ready to order?	**Bent u zover om te bestellen?** [bɛnt ju 'zɔvər ɔm tə bəs'tɛlən?]
What will you have?	**Wat wenst u?** [wat wɛnst ju?]
I'll have ...	**Voor mij ...** [vɔ:r mɛj ...]
I'm a vegetarian.	**Ik ben vegetariër.** [ik bɛn vexə'tarijər]
meat	**vlees** [vle:s]
fish	**vis** [vis]
vegetables	**groente** ['xruntə]
Do you have vegetarian dishes?	**Hebt u vegetarische gerechten?** [hɛpt ju vexə'tarisə xə'rɛxtən?]
I don't eat pork.	**Ik eet niet varkensvlees.** [ik e:t nit 'varkənsvle:s]
He /she/ doesn't eat meat.	**Hij /zij/ eet geen vlees.** [hɛj /zɛj/ e:t xe:n vle:s]

I am allergic to ...	**Ik ben allergisch voor ...** [ik bɛn ɑ'lerxis vɔ:r ...]
Would you please bring me ...	**Wil u mij ... brengen** [wil ju mɛj ... b'rɛŋən]
salt | pepper | sugar	**zout | peper | suiker** ['zɑut | 'pepər | 'sœykər]
coffee | tea | dessert	**koffie | thee | dessert** ['kɔfi | te: | dɛ'sɛ:r]
water | sparkling | plain	**water | met prik | gewoon** ['wɑtər | mɛt prik | xə'wɔ:n]
a spoon | fork | knife	**een lepel | vork | mes** [en 'lepəl | vɔrk | mɛs]
a plate | napkin	**een bord | servet** [en bɔrt | sɛr'vɛt]

Enjoy your meal!	**Smakelijk!** ['smɑkələk!]
One more, please.	**Nog een alstublieft.** [nɔx en ɑlsty'blift]
It was very delicious.	**Het was heerlijk.** [hɛt wɑs 'he:rlək]

---

check | change | tip	**rekening | wisselgeld | fooi** ['rekəniŋ | 'wisəl xɛlt | fɔ:j]
Check, please. (Could I have the check, please?)	**De rekening alstublieft.** [də 'rekəniŋ ɑlsty'blift]
Can I pay by credit card?	**Kan ik met een creditcard betalen?** [kɑn ik mɛt en 'kredit kɑrt bə'tɑlən?]
I'm sorry, there's a mistake here.	**Sorry, hier is een fout.** ['sɔri, hir iz en 'fɑut]

Shopping

Can I help you?	**Waarmee kan ik u van dienst zijn?** [wa:r'me: kan ik ju van dinst zɛjn?]
Do you have ...?	**Hebt u ...?** [hɛpt ju ...?]
I'm looking for ...	**Ik zoek ...** [ik zuk ...]
I need ...	**Ik heb ... nodig** [ik hɛp ... 'nɔdəx]
I'm just looking.	**Ik kijk even.** [ik kɛjk 'evən]
We're just looking.	**Wij kijken even.** [wɛj 'kɛjkən 'evən]
I'll come back later.	**Ik kom wat later terug.** [ik kɔm wat 'latər te'ryx]
We'll come back later.	**We komen later terug.** [we 'kɔmən 'latər te'ryx]
discounts | sale	**korting | uitverkoop** ['kɔrtiŋ | 'œytverkɔ:p]
Would you please show me ...	**Kunt u mij ... laten zien alstublieft?** [kynt ju mɛj ... 'latən zin alsty'blift?]
Would you please give me ...	**Kunt u mij ... geven alstublieft?** [kynt ju mɛj ... 'xevən alsty'blift?]
Can I try it on?	**Kan ik dit passen?** [kan ik dit 'pasən?]
Excuse me, where's the fitting room?	**Pardon, waar is de paskamer?** [par'dɔn, wa:r is də 'paskamər?]
Which color would you like?	**Welke kleur wenst u?** ['wɛlkə 'klør wɛnst ju?]
size | length	**maat | lengte** [ma:t | 'leŋtə]
How does it fit?	**Past het?** [past ət?]
How much is it?	**Hoeveel kost het?** ['huve:l kɔst ət?]
That's too expensive.	**Dat is te duur.** [dat is tə dy:r]
I'll take it.	**Ik neem het.** [ik ne:m ət]
Excuse me, where do I pay?	**Pardon, waar moet ik betalen?** [par'dɔn, wa:r mut ik bə'talən?]

Will you pay in cash or credit card?	**Betaalt u contant of met een creditcard?** [bə'ta:lt ju kɔn'tant ɔf mɛt en 'kredit kart?]
In cash | with credit card	**contant | met een creditcard** [kɔn'tant | mɛt en 'kredit kart]
Do you want the receipt?	**Wil u een kwitantie?** [wil ju en kwi'tantsi?]
Yes, please.	**Ja graag.** [ja xra:x]
No, it's OK.	**Nee, hoeft niet.** [ne:, huft nit]
Thank you. Have a nice day!	**Bedankt. Een fijne dag verder!** [bə'dankt. en 'fɛjnə dax 'vɛrdər!]

In town

Excuse me, please.	**Pardon, ...** [par'dɔn, ...]
I'm looking for ...	**Ik ben op zoek naar ...** [ik bɛn ɔp zuk na:r ...]
the subway	**de metro** [də 'metrɔ]
my hotel	**mijn hotel** [mɛjn hɔ'tɛl]
the movie theater	**de bioscoop** [də biɔ'skɔ:p]
a taxi stand	**een taxistandplaats** [en 'taksi 'stantpla:ʦ]
an ATM	**een geldautomaat** [en xɛlt autɔ'ma:t]
a foreign exchange office	**een wisselagent** [en 'wisəl a'xɛnt]
an internet café	**een internet café** [en 'intərnɛt ka'fe]
... street	**... straat** [... stra:t]
this place	**dit adres** [dit ad'rɛs]
Do you know where ... is?	**Weet u waar ... is?** [we:t ju wa:r ... is?]
Which street is this?	**Welke straat is dit?** ['wɛlkə stra:t is dit?]
Show me where we are right now.	**Kunt u me aanwijzen waar we nu zijn?** [kynt ju mə 'a:nwɛjzən wa:r wə ny zɛjn]
Can I get there on foot?	**Kan ik er lopend naar toe?** [kan ik ɛr 'lɔpənt na:r tu?]
Do you have a map of the city?	**Hebt u een plattegrond van de stad?** [hɛpt ju en platə'xrɔnt van də stat?]
How much is a ticket to get in?	**Hoeveel kost de toegang?** ['huve:l kɔst də 'tuxaŋ?]
Can I take pictures here?	**Kan ik hier foto's maken?** [kan ik hir 'fɔtɔs 'makən?]
Are you open?	**Bent u open?** [bɛnt ju 'ɔpən?]

When do you open?	**Hoe laat gaat u open?** [hu la:t xa:t ju 'ɔpən?]
When do you close?	**Hoe laat sluit u?** [hu la:t slœyt ju?]

Money

money	**geld** [xɛlt]
cash	**contant** [kɔn'tɑnt]
paper money	**bankbiljetten** [bɑnk bi'ʎetən]
loose change	**kleingeld** ['klɛjnxɛlt]
check | change | tip	**rekening | wisselgeld | fooi** ['rekəniŋ | 'wisəl xɛlt | fɔ:j]
credit card	**creditcard** ['kredit kɑrt]
wallet	**portemonnee** [pɔrtəmɔ'ne:]
to buy	**kopen** ['kɔpən]
to pay	**betalen** [bə'tɑlən]
fine	**boete** ['butə]
free	**gratis** ['xrɑtis]
Where can I buy …?	**Waar kan ik … kopen?** [wɑ:r kɑn ik … 'kɔpən?]
Is the bank open now?	**Is de bank nu open?** [is də bɑnk ny 'ɔpən?]
When does it open?	**Hoe laat gaat hij open?** [hu lɑ:t xɑ:t hɛj 'ɔpən?]
When does it close?	**Hoe laat sluit hij?** [hu lɑ:t slœyt hɛj?]
How much?	**Hoeveel?** ['huve:l?]
How much is this?	**Hoeveel kost dit?** ['huve:l kɔst dit?]
That's too expensive.	**Dat is te duur.** [dɑt is tə dy:r]
Excuse me, where do I pay?	**Pardon, waar moet ik betalen?** [pɑr'dɔn, wɑ:r mut ik bə'tɑlən?]
Check, please.	**De rekening alstublieft.** [də 'rekəniŋ ɑlsty'blift]

Can I pay by credit card?	**Kan ik met een creditcard betalen?** [kan ik mɛt en 'kredit kart bə'talən?]
Is there an ATM here?	**Is hier een geldautomaat?** [is hir en xɛlt autɔ'ma:t?]
I'm looking for an ATM.	**Ik zoek een geldautomaat.** [ik zuk en xɛlt autɔ'ma:t]

I'm looking for a foreign exchange office.	**Ik zoek een wisselagent.** [ik zuk en 'wisəl a'xɛnt]
I'd like to change ...	**Ik zou ... willen wisselen.** [ik 'zau ... 'wilən 'wisələn]
What is the exchange rate?	**Wat is de wisselkoers?** [wat is də 'wisəl kurs?]
Do you need my passport?	**Hebt u mijn paspoort nodig?** [hɛpt ju mɛjn 'paspɔ:rt 'nɔdəx?]

Time

What time is it?	**Hoe laat is het?** [hu la:t is ət?]
When?	**Wanneer?** [wa'ne:r?]
At what time?	**Hoe laat?** [hu la:t?]
now | later | after ...	**nu | later | na ...** [ny | 'latər | na ...]
one o'clock	**een uur** [en y:r]
one fifteen	**kwart over een** [kwart 'ɔvər en]
one thirty	**half twee** [half twe:]
one forty-five	**kwart voor twee** [kwart vɔ:r twe:]
one | two | three	**een | twee | drie** [en | twe: | dri]
four | five | six	**vier | vijf | zes** [vir | vɛjf | zɛs]
seven | eight | nine	**zeven | acht | negen** ['zevən | axt | 'nexən]
ten | eleven | twelve	**tien | elf | twaalf** [tin | ɛlf | twa:lf]
in ...	**binnen ...** ['binən ...]
five minutes	**vijf minuten** [vɛjf mi'nytən]
ten minutes	**tien minuten** [tin mi'nytən]
fifteen minutes	**vijftien minuten** ['vɛjftin mi'nytən]
twenty minutes	**twintig minuten** ['twintəx mi'nytən]
half an hour	**een half uur** [en half y:r]
an hour	**een uur** [en y:r]

in the morning	**s ochtends** [s 'ɔxtənts]
early in the morning	**s ochtends vroeg** [s 'ɔxtənts vrux]
this morning	**vanmorgen** [van'mɔrxən]
tomorrow morning	**morgenochtend** ['mɔrxən 'ɔxtənt]

at noon	**in het midden van de dag** [in ət 'midən van də dax]
in the afternoon	**s middags** [s 'midaxs]
in the evening	**s avonds** [s 'avɔnts]
tonight	**vanavond** [va'navɔnt]

at night	**s avonds** [s 'avɔnts]
yesterday	**gisteren** ['xistərən]
today	**vandaag** [van'da:x]
tomorrow	**morgen** ['mɔrxən]
the day after tomorrow	**overmorgen** [ɔvər'mɔrxən]

What day is it today?	**Wat is het vandaag?** [wat is ət van'da:x?]
It's ...	**Het is ...** [hɛt is ...]
Monday	**maandag** ['ma:ndax]
Tuesday	**dinsdag** ['dinzdax]
Wednesday	**woensdag** ['wunzdax]

Thursday	**donderdag** ['dɔndərdax]
Friday	**vrijdag** ['vrɛjdax]
Saturday	**zaterdag** ['zatərdax]
Sunday	**zondag** ['zɔndax]

Greetings. Introductions

Hello.	**Hallo.** ['halɔ]
Pleased to meet you.	**Aangenaam.** ['a:nxəna:m]
Me too.	**Insgelijks.** ['insxeləks]
I'd like you to meet ...	**Mag ik u voorstellen aan ...** [max ik ju 'vɔ:rstɛlən a:n ...]
Nice to meet you.	**Aangenaam.** ['a:nxəna:m]
How are you?	**Hoe gaat het met u?** [hu xa:t ət mɛt ju?]
My name is ...	**Ik heet ...** [ik he:t ...]
His name is ...	**Dit is ...** [dit is ...]
Her name is ...	**Dit is ...** [dit is ...]
What's your name?	**Hoe heet u?** [hu he:t ju?]
What's his name?	**Hoe heet hij?** [hu he:t hɛj?]
What's her name?	**Hoe heet zij?** [hu he:t zɛj?]
What's your last name?	**Wat is uw achternaam?** [wat is yw 'axtərna:m?]
You can call me ...	**Noem mij maar ...** [num mɛj ma:r ...]
Where are you from?	**Vanwaar komt u?** [van'wa:r kɔmt ju?]
I'm from ...	**Ik kom van ...** [ik kɔm van ...]
What do you do for a living?	**Wat is uw beroep?** [wat is yw bə'rup?]
Who is this?	**Wie is dit?** [wi is dit?]
Who is he?	**Wie is hij?** [wi is hɛj?]
Who is she?	**Wie is zij?** [wi is zɛj?]
Who are they?	**Wie zijn zij?** [wi zɛjn zɛj?]

This is ...	**Dit is ...** [dit is ...]
my friend (masc.)	**mijn vriend** [mɛjn vrint]
my friend (fem.)	**mijn vriendin** [mɛjn vrin'din]
my husband	**mijn man** [mɛjn man]
my wife	**mijn vrouw** [mɛjn 'vrau]

my father	**mijn vader** [mɛjn 'vadər]
my mother	**mijn moeder** [mɛjn 'mudər]
my brother	**mijn broer** [mɛjn brur]
my sister	**mijn zuster** [mɛjn 'zystər]
my son	**mijn zoon** [mɛjn zɔ:n]
my daughter	**mijn dochter** [mɛjn 'dɔxtər]

This is our son.	**Dit is onze zoon.** [dit is 'ɔnzə zɔ:n]
This is our daughter.	**Dit is onze dochter.** [dit is 'ɔnzə 'dɔxtər]
These are my children.	**Dit zijn mijn kinderen.** [dit zɛjn 'mɛjn 'kindərən]
These are our children.	**Dit zijn onze kinderen.** [dit zɛjn 'ɔnzə 'kindərən]

Farewells

Good bye!	**Tot ziens!** [tɔt zins!]
Bye! (inform.)	**Doei!** [dui!]
See you tomorrow.	**Tot morgen.** [tɔt 'mɔrxən]
See you soon.	**Tot binnenkort.** [tɔt binə'kɔrt]
See you at seven.	**Tot om zeven uur.** [tɔt ɔm 'zevən y:r]
Have fun!	**Veel plezier!** [ve:l plə'zi:r!]
Talk to you later.	**Tot straks.** [tɔt straks]
Have a nice weekend.	**Prettig weekend.** ['prɛtəx 'wi:kɛnt]
Good night.	**Goede nacht.** ['xudə naxt]
It's time for me to go.	**ik moet opstappen.** [ik mut 'ɔpstapən]
I have to go.	**Ik moet weg.** [ik mut wɛx]
I will be right back.	**ik ben zo terug.** [ik bɛn zɔ te'ryx]
It's late.	**Het is al laat.** [hɛt is al la:t]
I have to get up early.	**Ik moet vroeg op.** [ik mut vrux ɔp]
I'm leaving tomorrow.	**Ik vertrek morgen.** [ik vər'trɛk 'mɔrxən]
We're leaving tomorrow.	**Wij vertrekken morgen.** [wɛj vər'trɛkən 'mɔrxən]
Have a nice trip!	**Prettige reis!** ['prɛtixə rɛjs!]
It was nice meeting you.	**Het was fijn u te leren kennen.** [hɛt was fɛjn ju tə 'lerən 'kɛnən]
It was nice talking to you.	**Het was een prettig gesprek.** [hɛt was en 'prɛtəx xe'sprɛk]
Thanks for everything.	**Dank u wel voor alles.** [dank ju wɛl vɔ:r 'aləs]

I had a very good time.	**ik heb ervan genoten.** [ik hɛp ɛr'van xe'nɔtən]
We had a very good time.	**Wij hebben ervan genoten.** [wɛj 'hɛbən ɛr'van xe'nɔtən]
It was really great.	**Het was bijzonder leuk.** [hɛt was bi'zɔndər 'løk]
I'm going to miss you.	**Ik ga je missen.** [ik xa je 'misən]
We're going to miss you.	**Wij gaan je missen.** [wɛj xa:n je 'misən]

Good luck!	**Veel succes!** [ve:l syk'sɛs!]
Say hi to ...	**De groeten aan ...** [də 'xrutən a:n ...]

Foreign language

I don't understand.	**Ik versta het niet.** [ik vər'sta ət nit]
Write it down, please.	**Schrijf het neer alstublieft.** [sxrɛjf ət ne:r alsty'blift]
Do you speak ...?	**Spreekt u ...?** [spre:kt ju ...?]
I speak a little bit of ...	**Ik spreek een beetje ...** [ik spre:k en 'be:tʲə ...]
English	**Engels** ['ɛŋəls]
Turkish	**Turks** [tyrks]
Arabic	**Arabisch** [a'rabis]
French	**Frans** [frans]
German	**Duits** ['dœyts]
Italian	**Italiaans** [itali'a:ns]
Spanish	**Spaans** [spa:ns]
Portuguese	**Portugees** [pɔrty'xe:s]
Chinese	**Chinees** [ʃi'ne:s]
Japanese	**Japans** [ja'pans]
Can you repeat that, please.	**Kunt u dat herhalen alstublieft.** [kynt ju dat hɛr'halən alsty'blift]
I understand.	**Ik versta het.** [ik vər'sta ət]
I don't understand.	**Ik versta het niet.** [ik vər'sta ət nit]
Please speak more slowly.	**Spreek wat langzamer alstublieft.** [spre:k wat 'laŋzamər alsty'blift]
Is that correct? (Am I saying it right?)	**Is dat juist?** [is dat jœyst?]
What is this? (What does this mean?)	**Wat is dit?** [wat is dit?]

Apologies

Excuse me, please.	**Excuseer me alstublieft.** [ɛksky'ze:r mə ɑlsty'blift]
I'm sorry.	**Sorry.** ['sɔri]
I'm really sorry.	**Het spijt me.** [hɛt spɛjt mə]
Sorry, it's my fault.	**Sorry, het is mijn schuld.** ['sɔri, hɛt is mɛjn sxylt]
My mistake.	**Mijn schuld.** [mɛjn sxylt]

May I ...?	**Mag ik ...?** [mɑx ik ...?]
Do you mind if I ...?	**Is het goed dat ...?** [iz ət xut dɑt ...?]
It's OK.	**Het is okay.** [hɛt is ɔ'kɛj]
It's all right.	**Maakt niet uit.** [ma:kt nit œyt]
Don't worry about it.	**Maak je geen zorgen.** [ma:k je xe:n 'zɔrxən]

Agreement

Yes.	**Ja.** [ja]
Yes, sure.	**Ja zeker.** [ja 'zekər]
OK (Good!)	**Goed!** [xut!]
Very well.	**Uitstekend.** [œyt'stekənt]
Certainly!	**Zeker weten!** ['zekər 'wetən!]
I agree.	**Ik ga akkoord.** [ik xɑ ɑ'kɔ:rt]
That's correct.	**Precies.** [prə'sis]
That's right.	**Juist.** ['jœyst]
You're right.	**Je hebt gelijk.** [je hɛpt xə'lɛjk]
I don't mind.	**Ik doe het graag.** [ik du ət xrɑ:x]
Absolutely right.	**Dat is juist.** [dɑt is jœyst]
It's possible.	**Dat is mogelijk.** [dɑt is 'mɔxələk]
That's a good idea.	**Dat is een goed idee.** [dɑt is en xut i'de:]
I can't say no.	**Ik kan niet nee zeggen.** [ik kɑn nit ne: 'zɛxən]
I'd be happy to.	**Met genoegen.** [mɛt xə'nuxən]
With pleasure.	**Graag.** [xrɑ:x]

Refusal. Expressing doubt

No.	**Nee.** [ne:]
Certainly not.	**Beslist niet.** [bəs'list nit]
I don't agree.	**Daar ben ik het niet mee eens.** [da:r bɛn ik ət nit me: e:ns]
I don't think so.	**Dat geloof ik niet.** [dat xe'lɔ:f ik nit]
It's not true.	**Dat is niet waar.** [dat is nit wa:r]
You are wrong.	**U maakt een fout.** [ju ma:kt en 'faut]
I think you are wrong.	**Ik denk dat u een fout maakt.** [ik dɛnk dat ju en 'faut ma:kt]
I'm not sure.	**Ik weet het niet zeker.** [ik we:t ət nit 'zekər]
It's impossible.	**Het is onmogelijk.** [hɛt is ɔn'mɔxələk]
Nothing of the kind (sort)!	**Beslist niet!** [bəs'list nit!]
The exact opposite.	**Precies het tegenovergestelde!** [prə'sis hɛt 'texən 'ɔvərxəstɛldə!]
I'm against it.	**Ik ben er tegen.** [ik bɛn ɛr 'texən]
I don't care.	**Ik geef er niet om.** [ik xe:f ɛr nit ɔm]
I have no idea.	**Ik heb geen idee.** [ik hɛp xe:n i'de:]
I doubt that.	**Dat betwijfel ik.** [dat bet'wɛjfəl ik]
Sorry, I can't.	**Sorry, ik kan niet.** ['sɔri, ik kan nit]
Sorry, I don't want to.	**Sorry, ik wil niet.** ['sɔri, ik wil nit]
Thank you, but I don't need this.	**Dank u, maar ik heb dit niet nodig.** [dank ju, ma:r ik hɛp dit nit 'nɔdəx]
It's late.	**Het wordt laat.** [hɛt wɔrt la:t]

I have to get up early.	**Ik moet vroeg op.** [ik mut vrux ɔp]
I don't feel well.	**Ik voel me niet lekker.** [ik vul mə nit 'lɛkər]

Expressing gratitude

Thank you.	**Bedankt.** [bə'dankt]
Thank you very much.	**Heel erg bedankt.** [he:l ɛrx bə'dankt]
I really appreciate it.	**Ik stel dit zeer op prijs.** [ik stel dit ze:r ɔp prɛjs]
I'm really grateful to you.	**Ik ben u erg dankbaar.** [ik bɛn ju ɛrx 'dankba:r]
We are really grateful to you.	**Wij zijn u erg dankbaar.** [wɛj zɛjn ju ɛrx 'dankba:r]
Thank you for your time.	**Bedankt voor uw tijd.** [bə'dankt vɔ:r yw tɛjt]
Thanks for everything.	**Dank u wel voor alles.** [dank ju wɛl vɔ:r 'aləs]
Thank you for ...	**Bedankt voor ...** [bə'dankt vɔ:r ...]
your help	**uw hulp** [yw hylp]
a nice time	**een leuke dag** [en 'løkə dax]
a wonderful meal	**een heerlijke maaltijd** [en 'he:rlɛkə 'ma:ltɛjt]
a pleasant evening	**een prettige avond** [en 'prɛtixə 'avɔnt]
a wonderful day	**een prettige dag** [en 'prɛtixə dax]
an amazing journey	**een fantastische reis** [en fan'tastise rɛjs]
Don't mention it.	**Graag gedaan.** [xra:x xə'da:n]
You are welcome.	**Graag gedaan.** [xra:x xə'da:n]
Any time.	**Graag gedaan.** [xra:x xə'da:n]
My pleasure.	**Tot uw dienst.** [tɔt yw dinst]
Forget it. It's alright.	**Graag gedaan.** [xra:x xə'da:n]
Don't worry about it.	**Maak je geen zorgen.** [ma:k je xe:n 'zɔrxən]

Congratulations. Best wishes

Congratulations!	**Gefeliciteerd!** [xəfelisi'te:rt!]
Happy birthday!	**Gefeliciteerd met je verjaardag!** [xəfelisi'te:rt mɛt je və'rʲa:rdax!]
Merry Christmas!	**Prettig Kerstfeest!** ['prɛtəx 'kɛrstfe:st!]
Happy New Year!	**Gelukkig Nieuwjaar!** [xə'lykəx 'niu'ja:r!]
Happy Easter!	**Vrolijk Paasfeest!** ['vrɔlək 'pa:sfe:st!]
Happy Hanukkah!	**Gelukkig Chanoeka!** [xə'lykəx 'xanuka!]
I'd like to propose a toast.	**Ik wil een heildronk uitbrengen.** [ik wil en 'hɛjldrɔnk 'œytbreŋen]
Cheers!	**Proost!** [prɔ:st!]
Let's drink to ...!	**Laten we drinken op ...!** ['laten we 'drinkən ɔp ... !]
To our success!	**Op ons succes!** [ɔp ɔns syk'sɛs!]
To your success!	**Op uw succes!** [ɔp yw syk'sɛs!]
Good luck!	**Veel succes!** [ve:l syk'sɛs!]
Have a nice day!	**Een prettige dag!** [en 'prɛtixə dax!]
Have a good holiday!	**Een prettige vakantie!** [en 'prɛtixə va'kantsi!]
Have a safe journey!	**Een veilige reis!** [en 'vɛjlixə rɛjs!]
I hope you get better soon!	**Ik hoop dat u gauw weer beter bent!** [ik ho:p dat ju 'xau we:r 'betər bɛnt!]

Socializing

Why are you sad?	**Waarom zie je er zo verdrietig uit?** [wa:'rɔm zi je ɛr zɔ vər'dritəx œyt?]
Smile! Cheer up!	**Lach eens! Wees vrolijk!** [lax e:ns! we:s 'vrɔlək!]
Are you free tonight?	**Ben je vrij vanavond?** [bɛn je vrɛj va'navɔnt?]
May I offer you a drink?	**Mag ik je een drankje aanbieden?** [max ik je en 'drankje 'a:nbidən?]
Would you like to dance?	**Zullen we eens dansen?** ['zylən we e:ns 'dansən?]
Let's go to the movies.	**Laten we naar de bioscoop gaan.** ['latən we na:r də biɔ'skɔ:p xa:n]
May I invite you to ...?	**Mag ik je uitnodigen naar ...?** [max ik je 'œytnɔdixən na:r ...?]
a restaurant	**een restaurant** [en rɛstɔ'ran]
the movies	**de bioscoop** [də biɔ'skɔ:p]
the theater	**het theater** [hɛt te'ater]
go for a walk	**een wandeling** [en 'wandəliŋ]
At what time?	**Hoe laat?** [hu la:t?]
tonight	**vanavond** [va'navɔnt]
at six	**om zes uur** [ɔm zɛs y:r]
at seven	**om zeven uur** [ɔm 'zevən y:r]
at eight	**om acht uur** [ɔm axt y:r]
at nine	**om negen uur** [ɔm 'nexən y:r]
Do you like it here?	**Vind u het hier leuk?** [vint ju ət hir 'løk?]
Are you here with someone?	**Bent u hier met iemand?** [bɛnt ju hir mɛt i'mant?]
I'm with my friend.	**Ik ben met mijn vriend.** [ik bɛn mɛt mɛjn vrint]

I'm with my friends.	**Ik ben met mijn vrienden.** [ik bɛn mɛt mɛjn 'vrindən]
No, I'm alone.	**Nee, ik ben alleen.** [ik bɛn ɑ'le:n]
Do you have a boyfriend?	**Heb jij een vriendje?** [hɛp jɛj en 'vrindje?]
I have a boyfriend.	**Ik heb een vriendje.** [ik hɛp en 'vrindje]
Do you have a girlfriend?	**Heb jij een vriendin?** [hɛp jɛj en vrin'din?]
I have a girlfriend.	**Ik heb een vriendin.** [ik hɛp en vrin'din]
Can I see you again?	**Kan ik je weer eens zien?** [kɑn ik je we:r e:ns zin?]
Can I call you?	**Mag ik je opbellen?** [mɑx ik je ɔ'bɛlən?]
Call me. (Give me a call.)	**Bel me op.** [bɛl mə ɔp]
What's your number?	**Wat is je nummer?** [wɑt is je 'nymər?]
I miss you.	**Ik mis je.** [ik mis je]
You have a beautiful name.	**U hebt een mooie naam.** [ju hɛpt en mɔ:je nɑ:m]
I love you.	**Ik hou van jou.** [ik 'hɑu vɑn 'jɑu]
Will you marry me?	**Wil je met me trouwen?** [wil je mɛt mə 'trɑuwən?]
You're kidding!	**Dat meen je niet!** [dɑt me:n je nit!]
I'm just kidding.	**Grapje.** ['xrɑpje]
Are you serious?	**Meen je dat?** [me:n je dɑt?]
I'm serious.	**Ik meen het.** [ik me:n ət]
Really?!	**Heus waar?!** [høs wɑ:r?!]
It's unbelievable!	**Dat is ongelooflijk!** [dɑt is ɔnxə'lɔ:flək!]
I don't believe you.	**Ik geloof je niet.** [ik xə'lɔ:f je nit]
I can't.	**Ik kan niet.** [ik kɑn nit]
I don't know.	**Ik weet het niet.** [ik we:t ət nit]
I don't understand you.	**Ik versta u niet.** [ik vər'stɑ ju nit]

Please go away.	**Ga alstublieft weg.** [xa alsty'blift wɛx]
Leave me alone!	**Laat me gerust!** [la:t mə xə'ryst!]

I can't stand him.	**Ik kan hem niet uitstaan.** [ik kan hɛm nit 'œytsta:n]
You are disgusting!	**U bent een smeerlap!** [ju bɛnt en 'sme:rlap!]
I'll call the police!	**Ik ga de politie bellen!** [ik xa də pɔ'litsi 'bɛlən!]

Sharing impressions. Emotions

I like it.	**Dat vind ik fijn.** [dat vint ik fɛjn]
Very nice.	**Heel mooi.** [he:l mɔ:j]
That's great!	**Wat leuk!** [wat 'løk!]
It's not bad.	**Dat is niet slecht.** [dat is nit slɛxt]
I don't like it.	**Daar houd ik niet van.** [da:r 'haut ik nit van]
It's not good.	**Dat is niet goed.** [dat is nit xut]
It's bad.	**Het is slecht.** [hɛt is slɛxt]
It's very bad.	**Het is heel slecht.** [hɛt is he:l slɛxt]
It's disgusting.	**Het is smerig.** [hɛt is 'smerəx]
I'm happy.	**Ik ben blij.** [ik bɛn blɛj]
I'm content.	**Ik ben tevreden.** [ik bɛn təv'redən]
I'm in love.	**ik ben verliefd.** [ik bɛn vər'lift]
I'm calm.	**Ik voel me rustig.** [ik vul mə 'rystəx]
I'm bored.	**Ik verveel me.** [ik vər've:l mə]
I'm tired.	**Ik ben moe.** [ik bɛn mu]
I'm sad.	**Ik ben verdrietig.** [ik bɛn vər'dritəx]
I'm frightened.	**Ik ben bang.** [ik bɛn baŋ]
I'm angry.	**Ik ben kwaad.** [ik bɛn kwa:t]
I'm worried.	**Ik ben bezorgd.** [ik bɛn bə'zɔrxt]
I'm nervous.	**Ik ben zenuwachtig.** [ik bɛn 'zenywaxtəx]

I'm jealous. (envious)	**Ik ben jaloers.** [ik bɛn ja'lurs]
I'm surprised.	**Het verwondert me.** [hɛt vər'wɔndərt mə]
I'm perplexed.	**Ik sta paf.** [ik stɑ pɑf]

Problems. Accidents

I've got a problem.	**Ik heb een probleem.** [ik hɛp en prɔ'ble:m]
We've got a problem.	**Wij hebben een probleem.** [wɛj 'hɛbən en prɔ'ble:m]
I'm lost.	**Ik ben de weg kwijt.** [ik bɛn də wɛx kwɛjt]
I missed the last bus (train).	**Ik heb de laatste bus (trein) gemist.** [ik hɛp də 'la:tstə bys (trɛjn) xə'mist]
I don't have any money left.	**Ik heb geen geld meer.** [ik hɛp xe:n xɛlt me:r]
I've lost my ...	**Ik heb mijn ... verloren** [ik hɛp mɛjn ... vər'lɔrən]
Someone stole my ...	**Iemand heeft mijn ... gestolen** ['imant he:ft mɛjn ... xəs'tɔlən]
passport	**paspoort** ['paspɔ:rt]
wallet	**portemonnee** [pɔrtəmɔ'ne:]
papers	**papieren** [pa'pirən]
ticket	**kaartje** ['ka:rtʲə]
money	**geld** [xɛlt]
handbag	**tas** [tas]
camera	**camera** ['kamərа]
laptop	**laptop** ['lɛptɔp]
tablet computer	**tablet** [tab'lɛt]
mobile phone	**mobieltje** [mɔ'biltʲə]
Help me!	**Help!** [hɛlp!]
What's happened?	**Wat is er aan de hand?** [wat is ɛr a:n də hant?]
fire	**brand** [brant]

shooting	**er wordt geschoten** [ɛr wɔrt xəs'xɔtən]
murder	**moord** [mɔ:rt]
explosion	**ontploffing** [ɔntp'lɔfiŋ]
fight	**gevecht** [xə'vɛxt]

Call the police!	**Bel de politie!** [bɛl də pɔ'litsi!]
Please hurry up!	**Opschieten alstublieft!** ['ɔpsxitən alsty'blift!]
I'm looking for the police station.	**Ik zoek het politiebureau.** [ik zuk ət pɔ'litsi by'rɔ]
I need to make a call.	**Ik moet opbellen.** [ik mut ɔ'bɛlən]
May I use your phone?	**Mag ik uw telefoon gebruiken?** [max ik yw telə'fɔ:n xe'brœykən?]

I've been …	**Ik ben …** [ik bɛn …]
mugged	**overvallen** [ɔvər'valən]
robbed	**bestolen** [bəs'tɔlən]
raped	**verkracht** [vərk'raxt]
attacked (beaten up)	**aangevallen** ['a:nxəvalən]

Are you all right?	**Gaat het?** [xa:t ət?]
Did you see who it was?	**Hebt u gezien wie het was?** [hɛpt ju xə'zin wi ət was?]
Would you be able to recognize the person?	**Zou u de persoon kunnen herkennen?** ['zau ju də pɛr'sɔ:n 'kynən hɛr'kɛnən?]
Are you sure?	**Bent u daar zeker van?** [bɛnt ju da:r 'zekər van?]

Please calm down.	**Rustig aan alstublieft.** ['rystəx a:n alsty'blift]
Take it easy!	**Kalm aan!** [kalm a:n!]
Don't worry!	**Maak je geen zorgen!** [ma:k je xe:n 'zɔrxən!]
Everything will be fine.	**Alles komt in orde.** ['aləs kɔmt in 'ɔrdə]
Everything's all right.	**Alles is in orde.** ['aləs iz in 'ɔrdə]
Come here, please.	**Kom hier alstublieft.** [kɔm hir alsty'blift]

I have some questions for you.	**Ik heb een paar vragen voor u.** [ik hɛp en pa:r 'vraxən vɔ:r ju]
Wait a moment, please.	**Een ogenblikje alstublieft.** [en 'ɔxənblikjə alsty'blift]
Do you have any I.D.?	**Hebt u een ID-kaart?** [hɛpt ju en aj'di ka:rt?]
Thanks. You can leave now.	**Dank u. U mag nu vertrekken.** [dank ju. ju max ny vər'trɛkən]
Hands behind your head!	**Handen achter uw hoofd!** ['handən 'axtər yw hɔ:ft!]
You're under arrest!	**U bent onder arrest!** [ju bɛnt 'ɔndər a'rɛst!]

Health problems

Please help me.	**Kunt u mij helpen alstublieft?** [kynt ju mɛj 'hɛlpən alsty'blift]
I don't feel well.	**Ik voel me niet goed.** [ik vul mə nit xut]
My husband doesn't feel well.	**Mijn man voelt zich niet goed.** [mɛjn man vult zix nit xut]
My son ...	**Mijn zoon ...** [mɛjn zɔ:n ...]
My father ...	**Mijn vader ...** [mɛjn 'vadər ...]
My wife doesn't feel well.	**Mijn vrouw voelt zich niet goed.** [mɛjn 'vrau vult zix nit xut]
My daughter ...	**Mijn dochter ...** [mɛjn 'dɔxtər ...]
My mother ...	**Mijn moeder ...** [mɛjn 'mudər ...]
I've got a ...	**Ik heb ...** [ik hɛp ...]
headache	**hoofdpijn** ['hɔ:ftpɛjn]
sore throat	**keelpijn** ['ke:lpɛjn]
stomach ache	**maagpijn** ['ma:xpɛjn]
toothache	**tandpijn** ['tantpɛjn]
I feel dizzy.	**Ik voel me duizelig.** [ik vul mə 'dœyzələx]
He has a fever.	**Hij heeft koorts.** [hɛj he:ft kɔ:rts]
She has a fever.	**Zij heeft koorts.** [zɛj he:ft kɔ:rts]
I can't breathe.	**Ik heb moeite met ademen.** [ik hɛp 'mujtə mɛt 'adəmən]
I'm short of breath.	**Ik ben kortademig.** [ik bɛn kɔ'rtadəməx]
I am asthmatic.	**Ik ben astmatisch.** [ik bɛn astm'atis]
I am diabetic.	**Ik ben diabeet.** [ik bɛn 'diabe:t]

I can't sleep.	**Ik kan niet slapen.** [ik kan nit 'slapən]
food poisoning	**voedselvergiftiging** ['vuʦəl vər'xiftəxiŋ]

It hurts here.	**Het doet hier pijn.** [hɛt dut hir pɛjn]
Help me!	**Help!** [hɛlp!]
I am here!	**Ik ben hier!** [ik bɛn hir!]
We are here!	**Wij zijn hier!** [wɛj zɛjn hir!]
Get me out of here!	**Kom mij halen!** [kom mɛj 'halən!]
I need a doctor.	**Ik heb een dokter nodig.** [ik hɛp en 'dɔktər 'nɔdəx]
I can't move.	**Ik kan me niet bewegen.** [ik kan mə nit bə'wexən]
I can't move my legs.	**Ik kan mijn benen niet bewegen.** [ik kan mɛjn 'benən nit bə'wexən]

I have a wound.	**Ik heb een wond.** [ik hɛp en wɔnt]
Is it serious?	**Is het erg?** [iz ət ɛrx?]
My documents are in my pocket.	**Mijn documenten zijn in mijn zak.** [mɛjn dɔky'mɛntən zɛjn in mɛjn zak]
Calm down!	**Rustig maar!** ['rystəx ma:r!]
May I use your phone?	**Mag ik uw telefoon gebruiken?** [max ik yw telə'fɔ:n xə'brœykən?]

Call an ambulance!	**Bel een ambulance!** [bɛl en amby'lansə!]
It's urgent!	**Het is dringend!** [hɛt is 'driŋənt!]
It's an emergency!	**Het is een noodgeval!** [hɛt is en 'nɔ:txəval!]
Please hurry up!	**Opschieten alstublieft!** ['ɔpsxitən alsty'blift!]
Would you please call a doctor?	**Kunt u alstublieft een dokter bellen?** [kynt ju alsty'blift en 'dɔktər 'bɛlən?]
Where is the hospital?	**Waar is het ziekenhuis?** [wa:r iz ət 'zikənhœys?]

How are you feeling?	**Hoe voelt u zich?** [hu vult ju zix?]
Are you all right?	**Hoe gaat het?** [hu xa:t ət?]
What's happened?	**Wat is er gebeurd?** [wat is ɛr xə'børt?]

I feel better now.	**Ik voel me nu wat beter.** [ik vul mə ny wɑt 'betər]
It's OK.	**Het is okay.** [hɛt is ɔ'kɛj]
It's all right.	**Het gaat beter.** [hɛt xɑ:t 'betər]

At the pharmacy

pharmacy (drugstore)	**apotheek** [apɔ'te:k]
24-hour pharmacy	**dag en nacht apotheek** [dax en naxt apɔ'te:k]
Where is the closest pharmacy?	**Waar is de meest nabij gelegen apotheek?** [wa:r is də me:st na'bɛj xə'lexən apɔ'te:k?]
Is it open now?	**Is hij nu open?** [is hɛj ny 'ɔpən?]
At what time does it open?	**Hoe laat gaat hij open?** [hu la:t xa:t hɛj 'ɔpən?]
At what time does it close?	**Hoe laat sluit hij?** [hu la:t slœyt hɛj?]
Is it far?	**Is het ver?** [iz ət vɛr?]
Can I get there on foot?	**Kan ik er lopend naar toe?** [kan ik ɛr 'lopənt na:r tu?]
Can you show me on the map?	**Kunt u het op de plattegrond aanwijzen?** [kynt ju ət ɔp də plate'xrɔnt 'a:nwɛjzən?]
Please give me something for ...	**Geef mij alstublieft iets voor ...** [xe:f mɛj alsty'blift its vɔ:r ...]
a headache	**hoofdpijn** ['hɔ:ftpɛjn]
a cough	**hoest** [hust]
a cold	**verkoudheid** [vər'kauthɛjt]
the flu	**de griep** [də xrip]
a fever	**koorts** [kɔ:rts]
a stomach ache	**maagpijn** ['ma:xpɛjn]
nausea	**misselijkheid** ['misələkhɛjt]
diarrhea	**diarree** [dia're:]

constipation	**constipatie** [kɔnsti'patsi]
pain in the back	**rugpijn** ['ryxpɛjn]
chest pain	**pijn in mijn borst** [pɛjn in mɛjn bɔrst]
side stitch	**steek in de zij** [ste:k in də zɛj]
abdominal pain	**pijn in mijn onderbuik** [pɛjn in mɛjn 'ɔndərbœyk]

pill	**pil** [pil]
ointment, cream	**zalf, crème** [zalf, krɛ:m]
syrup	**stroop** [strɔ:p]
spray	**verstuiver** [vərstœyvər]
drops	**druppels** ['drypəls]

You need to go to the hospital.	**U moet naar het ziekenhuis.** [ju mut na:r ət 'zikənhœys]
health insurance	**ziektekostenverzekering** ['ziktəkɔstən vər'zekəriŋ]
prescription	**voorschrift** ['vɔ:rsxrift]
insect repellant	**anti-insecten middel** ['anti in'sɛktən 'midəl]
Band Aid	**pleister** ['plɛjstər]

The bare minimum

Excuse me, ...	**Pardon, ...** [par'dɔn, ...]
Hello.	**Hallo.** ['halɔ]
Thank you.	**Bedankt.** [bə'dankt]
Good bye.	**Tot ziens.** [tɔt zins]
Yes.	**Ja.** [ja]
No.	**Nee.** [ne:]
I don't know.	**Ik weet het niet.** [ik we:t ət nit]
Where? | Where to? | When?	**Waar? | Waarheen? | Wanneer?** [wa:r? | wa:r'he:n? | wa'ne:r?]
I need ...	**Ik heb ... nodig** [ik hɛp ... 'nɔdəx]
I want ...	**Ik wil ...** [ik wil ...]
Do you have ...?	**Hebt u ...?** [hɛpt ju ...?]
Is there a ... here?	**Is hier een ...?** [is hir en ...?]
May I ...?	**Mag ik ...?** [max ik ...?]
..., please (polite request)	**... alstublieft** [... alsty'blift]
I'm looking for ...	**Ik zoek ...** [ik zuk ...]
restroom	**toilet** [twa'lɛt]
ATM	**geldautomaat** [xɛlt autɔ'ma:t]
pharmacy (drugstore)	**apotheek** [apɔ'te:k]
hospital	**ziekenhuis** ['zikənhœys]
police station	**politiebureau** [pɔ'litsi by'rɔ]
subway	**metro** ['metrɔ]

taxi	**taxi** ['taksi]
train station	**station** [sta'sʲɔn]

My name is …	**Ik heet …** [ik he:t …]
What's your name?	**Hoe heet u?** [hu he:t ju?]
Could you please help me?	**Kunt u me helpen alstublieft?** [kynt ju mə 'hɛlpən alsty'blift?]
I've got a problem.	**Ik heb een probleem.** [ik hɛp en prɔ'ble:m]
I don't feel well.	**Ik voel me niet goed.** [ik vul mə nit xut]
Call an ambulance!	**Bel een ambulance!** [bɛl en amby'lansə!]
May I make a call?	**Mag ik opbellen?** [max ik ɔ'bɛlən?]

I'm sorry.	**Sorry.** ['sɔri]
You're welcome.	**Graag gedaan.** [xra:x xə'da:n]

I, me	**Ik, mij** [ik, mɛj]
you (inform.)	**jij** [jɛj]
he	**hij** [hɛj]
she	**zij** [zɛj]
they (masc.)	**zij** [zɛj]
they (fem.)	**zij** [zɛj]
we	**wij** [wɛj]
you (pl)	**jullie** ['juli]
you (sg, form.)	**u** [ju]

ENTRANCE	**INGANG** ['inxaŋ]
EXIT	**UITGANG** ['œytxaŋ]
OUT OF ORDER	**BUITEN GEBRUIK** ['bœytən xə'brœyk]
CLOSED	**GESLOTEN** [xə'slɔtən]

OPEN	**OPEN** ['ɔpən]
FOR WOMEN	**DAMES** ['daməs]
FOR MEN	**HEREN** ['herən]

MINI DICTIONARY

This section contains 250 useful words required for everyday communication. You will find the names of months and days of the week here. The dictionary also contains topics such as colors, measurements, family, and more

T&P Books Publishing

DICTIONARY CONTENTS

1. Time. Calendar 75
2. Numbers. Numerals 76
3. Humans. Family 77
4. Human body 78
5. Clothing. Personal accessories 79
6. House. Apartment 80

T&P Books Publishing

1. Time. Calendar

time	**tijd (de)**	[tεjt]
hour	**uur (het)**	[ju:r]
half an hour	**halfuur (het)**	[half 'ju:r]
minute	**minuut (de)**	[mi'ny:t]
second	**seconde (de)**	[se'kɔndə]
today (adv)	**vandaag**	[van'da:x]
tomorrow (adv)	**morgen**	['mɔrxən]
yesterday (adv)	**gisteren**	['xistərən]
Monday	**maandag (de)**	['ma:ndax]
Tuesday	**dinsdag (de)**	['dinsdax]
Wednesday	**woensdag (de)**	[ʋ'unsdax]
Thursday	**donderdag (de)**	['dɔndərdax]
Friday	**vrijdag (de)**	[v'rεjdax]
Saturday	**zaterdag (de)**	['zatərdax]
Sunday	**zondag (de)**	['zɔndax]
day	**dag (de)**	[dax]
working day	**werkdag (de)**	[ʋ'εrkdax]
public holiday	**feestdag (de)**	['fe:stdax]
weekend	**weekend (het)**	[ʋ'ikənt]
week	**week (de)**	[ʋe:k]
last week (adv)	**vorige week**	['vɔrixə ʋe:k]
next week (adv)	**volgende week**	['vɔlxəndə ʋe:k]
in the morning	**'s morgens**	[s 'mɔrxəns]
in the afternoon	**'s middags**	[s 'midax]
in the evening	**'s avonds**	[s 'avɔnts]
tonight (this evening)	**vanavond**	[va'navɔnt]
at night	**'s nachts**	[s naxts]
midnight	**middernacht (de)**	['midərnaxt]
January	**januari (de)**	[jany'ari]
February	**februari (de)**	[febry'ari]
March	**maart (de)**	[ma:rt]
April	**april (de)**	[ap'ril]
May	**mei (de)**	[mεj]
June	**juni (de)**	['juni]
July	**juli (de)**	['juli]
August	**augustus (de)**	[au'xystys]

September	**september (de)**	[sɛp'tɛmbər]
October	**oktober (de)**	[ɔk'tɔbər]
November	**november (de)**	[nɔ'vɛmbər]
December	**december (de)**	[de'sɛmbər]
in spring	**in de lente**	[in də 'lɛntə]
in summer	**in de zomer**	[in də 'zɔmər]
in fall	**in de herfst**	[in də hɛrfst]
in winter	**in de winter**	[in də ʊ'intər]
month	**maand (de)**	[ma:nt]
season (summer, etc.)	**seizoen (het)**	[sɛj'zun]
year	**jaar (het)**	[ja:r]

2. Numbers. Numerals

0 zero	**nul**	[nyl]
1 one	**een**	[en]
2 two	**twee**	[tʊe:]
3 three	**drie**	[dri]
4 four	**vier**	[vir]
5 five	**vijf**	[vɛjf]
6 six	**zes**	[zɛs]
7 seven	**zeven**	['zevən]
8 eight	**acht**	[ɑxt]
9 nine	**negen**	['nexən]
10 ten	**tien**	[tin]
11 eleven	**elf**	[ɛlf]
12 twelve	**twaalf**	[tʊa:lf]
13 thirteen	**dertien**	['dɛrtin]
14 fourteen	**veertien**	['ve:rtin]
15 fifteen	**vijftien**	['vɛjftin]
16 sixteen	**zestien**	['zɛstin]
17 seventeen	**zeventien**	['zevəntin]
18 eighteen	**achttien**	['ɑxtin]
19 nineteen	**negentien**	['nexəntin]
20 twenty	**twintig**	[tʊ'intəx]
30 thirty	**dertig**	['dɛrtəx]
40 forty	**veertig**	['ve:rtəx]
50 fifty	**vijftig**	['vɛjftəx]
60 sixty	**zestig**	['zɛstəx]
70 seventy	**zeventig**	['zevəntəx]
80 eighty	**tachtig**	['tɑhtəx]
90 ninety	**negentig**	['nexəntəx]
100 one hundred	**honderd**	['hɔndərt]

200 two hundred	**tweehonderd**	[tʊe: 'hɔndərt]
300 three hundred	**driehonderd**	[dri 'hɔndərt]
400 four hundred	**vierhonderd**	[vir 'hɔndərt]
500 five hundred	**vijfhonderd**	[vɛjf 'hɔndərt]
600 six hundred	**zeshonderd**	[zɛs 'hɔndərt]
700 seven hundred	**zevenhonderd**	['zevən 'hɔndərt]
800 eight hundred	**achthonderd**	[ɑxt 'hɔndərt]
900 nine hundred	**negenhonderd**	['nexən 'hɔndərt]
1000 one thousand	**duizend**	[dœyzənt]
10000 ten thousand	**tienduizend**	[tin dœyzənt]
one hundred thousand	**honderdduizend**	['hɔndərt dœyzənt]
million	**miljoen (het)**	[mi'ʎun]
billion	**miljard (het)**	[mi'ʎart]

3. Humans. Family

man (adult male)	**man (de)**	[mɑn]
young man	**jongen (de)**	['joŋən]
woman	**vrouw (de)**	[v'rɑu]
girl (young woman)	**meisje (het)**	['mɛjɕə]
old man	**oude man (de)**	['ɑudə mɑn]
old woman	**oude vrouw (de)**	['ɑudə v'rɑu]
mother	**moeder (de)**	['mudər]
father	**vader (de)**	['vɑdər]
son	**zoon (de)**	[zɔ:n]
daughter	**dochter (de)**	['dɔxtər]
brother	**broer (de)**	[brur]
sister	**zuster (de)**	['zystər]
parents	**ouders**	['ɑudərs]
child	**kind (het)**	[kint]
children	**kinderen**	['kindərən]
stepmother	**stiefmoeder (de)**	[s'tifmudər]
stepfather	**stiefvader (de)**	[s'tifvɑdər]
grandmother	**oma (de)**	['ɔmɑ]
grandfather	**opa (de)**	['ɔpɑ]
grandson	**kleinzoon (de)**	[klɛjn zɔ:n]
granddaughter	**kleindochter (de)**	[klɛjn 'dɔxtər]
grandchildren	**kleinkinderen**	[klɛjn 'kinderən]
uncle	**oom (de)**	[ɔ:m]
aunt	**tante (de)**	['tɑntə]
nephew	**neef (de)**	[ne:f]
niece	**nicht (de)**	[nixt]
wife	**vrouw (de)**	[v'rɑu]

husband	**man (de)**	[man]
married (masc.)	**gehuwd**	[xə'hyʊt]
married (fem.)	**gehuwd**	[xə'hyʊt]
widow	**weduwe (de)**	[ʊ'edyʊə]
widower	**weduwnaar (de)**	[ʊ'edyʊna:r]
name (first name)	**naam (de)**	[na:m]
surname (last name)	**achternaam (de)**	['axtərna:m]
relative	**familielid (het)**	[fa'mililit]
friend (masc.)	**vriend (de)**	[vrint]
friendship	**vriendschap (de)**	[v'rintsxap]
partner	**partner (de)**	['partnər]
superior (n)	**baas (de)**	[ba:s]
colleague	**collega (de)**	[kɔ'lexa]
neighbors	**buren**	['byrən]

4. Human body

body	**lichaam (het)**	['lixa:m]
heart	**hart (het)**	[hart]
blood	**bloed (het)**	[blut]
brain	**hersenen**	['hɛrsənən]
bone	**been (het)**	[be:n]
spine (backbone)	**ruggengraat (de)**	['ryxəxra:t]
rib	**rib (de)**	[rib]
lungs	**longen**	['lɔŋən]
skin	**huid (de)**	[hœyt]
head	**hoofd (het)**	[hɔ:ft]
face	**gezicht (het)**	[xə'ziht]
nose	**neus (de)**	['nøs]
forehead	**voorhoofd (het)**	['vɔ:rhɔ:ft]
cheek	**wang (de)**	[ʊaŋ]
mouth	**mond (de)**	[mɔnt]
tongue	**tong (de)**	[tɔŋ]
tooth	**tand (de)**	[tant]
lips	**lippen**	['lipən]
chin	**kin (de)**	[kin]
ear	**oor (het)**	[ɔ:r]
neck	**hals (de)**	[hals]
eye	**oog (het)**	[ɔ:x]
pupil	**pupil (de)**	[py'pil]
eyebrow	**wenkbrauw (de)**	[ʊ'ɛnkbrau]
eyelash	**wimper (de)**	[ʊ'impər]
hair	**haren**	['harən]

hairstyle	**kapsel (het)**	['kapsəl]
mustache	**snor (de)**	[snɔr]
beard	**baard (de)**	[ba:rt]
to have (a beard, etc.)	**dragen**	[d'raxən]
bald (adj)	**kaal**	[ka:l]
hand	**hand (de)**	[hant]
arm	**arm (de)**	[arm]
finger	**vinger (de)**	['viŋər]
nail	**nagel (de)**	['naxəl]
palm	**handpalm (de)**	['hantpalm]
shoulder	**schouder (de)**	[s'xaudər]
leg	**been (het)**	[be:n]
knee	**knie (de)**	[kni]
heel	**hiel (de)**	[hil]
back	**rug (de)**	[ryx]

5. Clothing. Personal accessories

clothes	**kleren** (mv.), **kleding (de)**	[k'lerən], [k'lediŋ]
coat (overcoat)	**jas (de)**	[jas]
fur coat	**bontjas (de)**	[bɔnt jas]
jacket (e.g., leather ~)	**jasje (het)**	['jaɕə]
raincoat (trenchcoat, etc.)	**regenjas (de)**	['rexən jas]
shirt (button shirt)	**overhemd (het)**	['ɔvərhɛmt]
pants	**broek (de)**	[bruk]
suit jacket	**colbert (de)**	['kɔlbər]
suit	**kostuum (het)**	[kɔs'ty:m]
dress (frock)	**jurk (de)**	[jurk]
skirt	**rok (de)**	[rɔk]
T-shirt	**T-shirt (het)**	['ti'ʃøt]
bathrobe	**badjas (de)**	['batʰjas]
pajamas	**pyjama (de)**	[pi'jama]
workwear	**werkkleding (de)**	[ʊ'ɛrk k'lediŋ]
underwear	**ondergoed (het)**	['ɔndərxut]
socks	**sokken**	['sɔkən]
bra	**beha (de)**	[be'ha]
pantyhose	**panty (de)**	['pɛnti]
stockings (thigh highs)	**nylonkousen**	['nɛjlɔn 'kausən]
bathing suit	**badpak (het)**	['badpak]
hat	**hoed (de)**	[hut]
footwear	**schoeisel (het)**	[s'xuisəl]
boots (cowboy ~)	**laarzen**	['la:rzən]
heel	**hiel (de)**	[hil]
shoestring	**veter (de)**	['vetər]

shoe polish	**schoensmeer (de/het)**	[s'xunsme:r]
gloves	**handschoenen**	['xantsxunən]
mittens	**wanten**	[ʋ'antən]
scarf (muffler)	**sjaal (de)**	[ɕa:l]
glasses (eyeglasses)	**bril (de)**	[bril]
umbrella	**paraplu (de)**	[parap'ly]
tie (necktie)	**das (de)**	[das]
handkerchief	**zakdoek (de)**	['zagduk]
comb	**kam (de)**	[kam]
hairbrush	**haarborstel (de)**	[ha:r 'bɔrstəl]
buckle	**gesp (de)**	[xɛsp]
belt	**broekriem (de)**	[b'rukrim]
purse	**damestas (de)**	['daməstas]

6. House. Apartment

apartment	**appartement (het)**	[apartə'mɛnt]
room	**kamer (de)**	['kamər]
bedroom	**slaapkamer (de)**	[s'la:pkamər]
dining room	**eetkamer (de)**	[e:t'kamər]
living room	**salon (de)**	[sa'lɔn]
study (home office)	**studeerkamer (de)**	[stu'de:r 'kamər]
entry room	**gang (de)**	[xaŋ]
bathroom (room with a bath or shower)	**badkamer (de)**	['batkamər]
half bath	**toilet (het)**	[tua'lɛt]
vacuum cleaner	**stofzuiger (de)**	[s'tɔfzœyxər]
mop	**zwabber (de)**	[zʋ'abər]
dust cloth	**poetsdoek (de)**	['putsduk]
short broom	**veger (de)**	['vexər]
dustpan	**stofblik (het)**	[s'tɔfblik]
furniture	**meubels**	['møbəl]
table	**tafel (de)**	['tafəl]
chair	**stoel (de)**	[stul]
armchair	**fauteuil (de)**	[fɔ'tøj]
mirror	**spiegel (de)**	[s'pixəl]
carpet	**tapijt (het)**	[ta'pɛjt]
fireplace	**haard (de)**	[ha:rt]
drapes	**gordijnen**	[xɔr'dɛjnən]
table lamp	**bureaulamp (de)**	[by'rɔlamp]
chandelier	**luchter (de)**	['lyxtər]
kitchen	**keuken (de)**	['køkən]
gas stove (range)	**gasfornuis (het)**	[xas fɔrnœys]

electric stove	**elektrisch fornuis (het)**	[ɛ'lɛktris fɔrnœys]
microwave oven	**magnetronoven (de)**	['mahnətrɔn 'ɔvən]
refrigerator	**koelkast (de)**	['kulkast]
freezer	**diepvriezer (de)**	[dipv'rizər]
dishwasher	**vaatwasmachine (de)**	['va:tʋas ma'ʃinə]
faucet	**kraan (de)**	[kra:n]
meat grinder	**vleesmolen (de)**	[v'le:smɔlən]
juicer	**vruchtenpers (de)**	[v'ryxtənpɛrs]
toaster	**toaster (de)**	['tɔ:stər]
mixer	**mixer (de)**	['miksər]
coffee machine	**koffiemachine (de)**	['kɔfima'ʃinə]
kettle	**fluitketel (de)**	[flœyt 'ketəl]
teapot	**theepot (de)**	['te:pɔt]
TV set	**televisie (de)**	[telə'vizi]
VCR (video recorder)	**videorecorder (de)**	['videɔ re'kɔrdər]
iron (e.g., steam ~)	**strijkijzer (het)**	[st'rɛjkɛjzər]
telephone	**telefoon (de)**	[telə'fɔ:n]

15287160R00048

Printed in Poland
by Amazon Fulfillment
Poland Sp. z o.o., Wrocław